THE LITTLE BOOK OF BLISS
The Perfect Antidote to Gloom

We are all in the gutter,
but some of us are looking at the stars

Oscar Wilde, 1854–1900

THE LITTLE BOOK OF BLISS

The Perfect Antidote to Gloom

MADELINE SWAN

Published in the United Kingdom in 2009
by Little Books Limited, London W11 3QP

10 9 8 7 6 5 4 3 2 1

Copyright 2009 by Madeline Swann

All rights reserved. No part of this work may be reproduced or utilised in any form or by any means, electronic or mechanical, including photocopying, recording or by any information, storage and retrieval system, without the prior written permission of the publisher.

A CIP catalogue record for this book is available from the British Library.

ISBN 978 1 906264 04 8

Printed in the UK by CPI Bookmarque, Croydon, CR0 4TD

Fed up? Cheesed off? Feeling jinxed? This book is designed to lift your mood and leave you grinning, if not chuckling. From time immemorial men and women have been in search of bliss. For writer Dostoyevsky in 19th century Russia it was children. For actress Emma Thompson it is Golden Wonder crisps. Woody Allen prefers sex.

Within these pages you'll find a hundred different definitions of the state of bliss, some sublime, some tongue in cheek, some downright naughty and all designed to cheer. Happy reading.

If you have two pennies, spend one on a loaf of bread and one on a flower. The bread will give you life and the flower will give you a reason for living.

Chinese Proverb

In my day – that is to say, during my main crisp-eating years – my dream of bliss was a packet of Golden Wonder Cheese & Onion. Now that's a crisp. It's a crisp because it's exactly what it says it is: it's crisp. But a packet of these doesn't make you bleed or need to lie down. Granted, you are less likely to be in for a snog afterwards, but for goodness' sake, are we to expect all pleasures at once?

Emma Thompson, 1959–

Let not the enjoyment of pleasures now within your grasp, be carried to such excess as to incapacitate you from future repetition.

Seneca c.4 BC–AD 65

Abstainer: A weak person who yields to the temptation of denying himself a pleasure.

Ambrose Bierce, 1842–1914

The discovery of a new dish does more for human happiness than the discovery of a new star.

Anthelme Brillat-Savarin, 1855-1926

I refuse to spend my life worrying about what I eat. There is no pleasure worth forgoing just for an extra three years in the geriatric ward.

John Mortimer

I am not a glutton
– I am an explorer of food.

Erma Bombeck, 1927–1996

My idea of ecstasy is to be smeared in
chocolate but a handsome man, then
left alone to lick it all off.

Jo Brand, 1957–

Madam, I have been looking for a person who disliked gravy all my life; let us swear eternal friendship.

Sydney Smith, 1771-1845

Part of the secret of success in life is to eat what you like and let the food fight it out inside.

Mark Twain, 1835–1910

Sex is good,
but not as good
as fresh sweet corn

Garrison Keller, 1942–

Oh, God above, if heaven has a taste it must be an egg with butter and salt, and after the egg is there anything in the world lovlier than fresh warm bread and a mug of sweet golden tea?

Frank McCourt, 1930–

It's good to be just plain happy. It's a little better to know that you're happy; but to understand that you're happy and to know why and how and still be happy — be happy in the being and the knowing — well, that is beyond happiness, that is bliss.

Henry Miller, 1891–1980

Ecstasy is a glass full of tea and a piece of sugar in the mouth.

Alexander Puskin, 1799–1837

My advice to you is not to inquire why or whither, but just to enjoy your ice cream while it's on your plate – that's my philosophy.

Thorton Wilder, 1897–1975

Prostitutes for pleasure, concubines for services, wives for breeding and a melon for ecstasy.

Richard Burton, 1821–90

To eat is human; to digest, divine.

Herbert Agar, 1897–1980

Everything has an end, except for the sausage, which has two.

Austrian saying

All happiness depends
on a leisurely breakfast

John Gunther, 1926–1992

When the insects take over the world, we hope they will remember with gratitude how we took them along on all our picnics.

Bill Vaughan, 1915–77

A Drink With Something In It

There is something about a martini,
A tingle remarkably pleasant;
A yellow, a mellow martini;
I wish I had one at present.
There is something about a martini,
Ere the dining and dancing begin,
And to tell you the truth,
It is not the vermouth —
I think that perhaps it's the gin.

Ogden Nash, 1902–1971

Our lager,
Which arts in barrels,
Hallowed be thy drink,
Thy will be drunk,
I will be drunk,
At home as in the tavern,
Give us this day our foamy head,
And forgive us our spilages,
As we forgive those who spill against us,
And lead us not into carnation,
But deliver us from hangovers,
For thine is the beer,
The bitter and the lager forever and ever

If it wasn't for coffee, I'd have no discernible personality at all.

David Letterman, 1947–

The rapturous, wild and ineffable
pleasure of drinking at someone
else's expense.

H. S. Leigh, 1870–1924

When I read about
the evils of drinking,
I gave up reading.

Hugh Youngman, 1842–1906

I have taken more out of alcohol than alcohol has ever taken out of me

Winston Churchill, 1874–1965

Beer is proof that God loves us and
wants us to be happy.

Benjamin Franklin, 1706–90

This coffee falls into your stomach, and straightway there is a general commotion. Ideas begin to move like the battalions of the Grand Army of the battlefield, and the battle takes place. Things remembered arrive at full gallop, ensuing to the wind. The light cavalry of comparisons deliver a magnificent deploying charge, the artillery of logic hurry up with their train and ammunition, the shafts of with start up like sharpshooters. Similes arise, the paper is covered with ink; for the struggle commences and is concluded with torrents of black water, just as a battle with powder.

Honoré de Balzac, 1799–1850

Every time you smile at someone,
it is an action of love, a gift to that
person, a beautiful thing.

Mother Theresa, 1910-97

One of the things I learnt when I was negotiating was that until I changed myself I could not change others.

Nelson Mandela, 1918–

Beware of desperate steps. The darkest
day will have passed away.

William Cowper, 1910–,
The Needless Alarm

Everything you can imagine is real.

Pablo Picasso, 1881–1973

If you have one true friend and are one to another you will double your joy and divide. your grief.

Irish proverb

We have fewer friends than we imagine,
but more than we know.

Huon von Hofmannsthal, 1874–1929

Visits always give pleasure, if not the arrival, the departure.

Portuguese proverb

I reckon being ill as one of the greatest pleasures of life, provided one is not too ill and is not obliged to work until one is better.

Samuel Butler,
The Way of All Flesh, *1835–1902*

I am pretty sure that, if you will be quite honest, you will admit that a good rousing sneeze, one that tears open your collar and throws your hair into your eyes, is really one of life's sensational pleasures.

Robert Benchley, 1889–1945

A clown is like an aspirin,
only he works twice as fast.

Groucho Marx, 1890–1977

I have been accustomed for some time past, to apply leeches to the inflamed testicle, which practice has always been followed with the most happy effects.

William Buchan, 1748–1812

You ask me what we need to win this war. I answer tobacco as much as bullets. Tobacco is as indispensable as the daily ration; we must have thousands of tons without delay.

General John J. Pershing, 1860–1948

Is the noble Lord aware that, at the age of 80, there are very few pleasures left to me, but one of them is passive smoking?

Baroness Trumpington,
House of Lords, 2003

Life is a gamble. You can get hurt, but people die in plane crashes, lose their arms and legs in car accidents; people die every day. Same with fighters, some die, some get hurt, some go on. You just don't let yourself believe it will happen to you.

Muhammad Ali, 1942–

If you feel that life is one of
God's jokes, there is still no
reason why we shouldn't make
it a good joke.

Kenneth Williams, 1926–99

Angels can fly because they take themselves lightly.

G.K. Chesterton, 1874–1936

There is nothing ugly; I never saw an ugly thing in my life: for let the form of an object be what it may, light, shade, and perspective will always make it beautiful.

John Constable, 1776–1837

There is more felicity on the far side of baldness than young men can possibly imagine.

Logan Pearsall Smith, Afterthoughts, *1931*

A thing of beauty is a joy for ever:
Its loveliness increases, it will never
Pass into nothingness, but still will keep
A bower quiet for us, and a sleep
Full of dreams, and health, and quiet breathing.

John Keats, Endymion, *1818*

The whole pleasure of marriage is to accept it is a perpetual crisis.

Anon.

Happiness? A good cigar, a good meal ... and a good woman ... or a bad woman, it depends on how much happiness you can handle.

George Burns, 1896–1996

Pleasure is the beginning
and the goal of a happy life.

Epicurus, 341–270 BC

A thick skin
is a gift from God.

Konrad Adenaeur, 1902–1994

Even God cannot change the past.

Agathon, 445–400BC

How can a man who has once strayed into Heaven ever hope to make terms with earth?

Alain-Fournier, 1886–1914

The way I look at it, you should live every day as if it were your birthday

Paris Hilton, 1981–

If you obey all the rules,
you miss all the fun

Katherine Hepburn, 1907–2003

There is no pleasure in having nothing to do; the fun is having lots to do and not doing it

Andrew Jackson, 1767–1845

Do not confuse relaxation with
laziness or inertia

Richard Hittleman, 1842–1897

Make it a rule of life never to regret and never to look back. Regret is an appalling waste of energy: you can't build on it: it's good only for wallowing in.

Katherine Mansfield, 1888–1923

Now, I don't want to get off on a rant here, but guilt is simply God's way of letting you know that you're having too good a time.

Dennis Miller, 1953–

A lie is an abomination unto the Lord
but a very present help in trouble.

Anon

If I have faltered more or less
In my great task of happiness
If I have moved among my race
And shown no glorious morning face;
If beams from happy human eyes
Have moved me not; if morning skies'
Books and my food and summer Rain
Knocked on my sullen heart in vain-
Lord, thy most pointed pleasure take
And stab my spirit broad awake.

Robert Louis Stevenson, 1850–1894

Is it so small a thing
to have enjoyed the sun,
To have lived light in the spring,
To have loved,
To have thought,
To have done?

Matthew Arnold,
The Hymn of Empedocles, *1852*

The Bright Field

I have seen the sun break through
to illuminate a small field
for a while, and gone my wayand forgotten it.
But that was the pearl
of great price, the one field that had
treasure in it. I realise now
that I must give all that I have
to possess it. Life is not hurrying

on to a receding future, nor hankering after
an imagined past. It is the turning
aside like Moses to the miracle
of the lit bush, to a brightness
that seemed as transitory as your youth
once, but is the eternity that awaits you.

R.S. Thomas, 1913–2000

Happy the man, and happy he alone,
He, who can call today his own;
He who, secure within, can say,
Tomorrow do thy worst, for I have
lived today.

John Dryden, Horace, III, xxix

The Peace of Wild Things

When despair for the world grows in me
and I wake in the night at the least sound
in fear of what my life and my children's lives
may be,
I go and lie down where the wood drake
rests in his beauty on the water, and the great
heron feeds.
I come into the peace of wild things
who do not tax their lives with forethought
of grief. I come to the presence of still water.
And I feel above me the day-blind stars
waiting with their light. For a time
I am rest in the grace of the world,
and am free.

Wendell Berry, 1934–

If we could see the miracle of a single flower clearly, our whole life would change.

Buddha

The best things in life are nearest: Breath in your nostrils, light in your eyes, flowers at your feet, duties at your hand, the path of right just before you. Then do not grasp at the stars, but do life's plain, common work as it comes, certain that daily duties and daily bread are the sweetest things in life.

Robert Louis Stevenson, 1850–1894

When I go out into the countryside and see the sun and the green and everything flowering, I say to myself 'Yes indeed, all that belongs to me!'

Henri Rousseau, 1844–1910

Pleasure for one hour, a bottle of wine. Pleasure for one year a marriage; but pleasure for a lifetime, a garden.

Chinese Proverb

The tree which moves some to tears of joy is in the eyes of others only a green thing that stands in the way. Some see nature all ridicule and deformity and some scarce see nature at all. But to the eyes of the man of imagination, nature is imagination itself.

William Blake, 1757–1827

Let children walk with Nature,
let them see the beautiful
blendings and communions
of death and life, their joyous
inseparable unity, as taught in
woods and meadows, plains and
mountains and streams of our
blessed star, and they will learn
that death is stingless indeed,
and as beautiful as life.

John Muir, 1838–1914

There was a time when meadow,
grove and stream,
To earth, and every common sight
To me did seem
Apparelled in celestial light,
The glory and the freshness of
a dream.

William Wordsworth, 1770–1850
Ode on Intimations of Immorality

I tend to believe that cricket is the greatest thing that God ever created on Earth . . . certainly better than sex although sex isn't too bad either. But everyone knows which comes first when it's a question of cricket or sex.

Harold Pinter, 1930–

Physical pleasure is a sensual experience no different from pure seeing or the pure sensation with which a fine fruit fills the tongue; it is a great unending experience, which is given us, a knowing of the world, the fullness and the glory of all knowing. And not our acceptance of it is bad; the bad thing is that most people misuse and squander this experience and apply it as a stimulant at the tired spots of their lives and as distraction instead of a rallying toward exalted moments.

Rainer Marja Rilke, 1875–1926

Sex without love is a meaningless experience, but as far as meaningless experiences go its pretty damn good.

Woody Allen, 1935–

Love is the answer, but while you're waiting for the answer, sex raises some good questions.

Woody Allen, 1935–

I have a simple principle for the conduct of life – never to resist an adequate temptation.

Max Lerner, 1902–1992

Abstainer: A weak person who yields to the temptation of denying himself a pleasure.

Ambrose Bierce, 1842–1914

Life affords no higher pleasure than that of sumounting difficulties, passing from one step of success to another, forming new wishes and seeing them gratified.

Samuel Johnson, 1709–1784

The good thing about masturbation is you don't have to dress up for it

Truman Capote, 1924–1984

Come sleep, O sleep,
the certain
knot of peace,
The baiting place of wit,
the balm of woe,
The poor man's wealth,
the prisoner's release,
The indifferent judge between the
high and low

Sir Philip Sidney,
Astrophel and Stella, *1591*

Whatever we may say, the happiest moment of the happy man is that of his falling asleep, just as the unhappiest moment of the unhappy man is that of his awakening.

Arthur Schopenhauer,
The World as Will and Representation,
1844

Blessings on him who invented sleep, the mantle that covers all human thoughts, the food that satisfies hunger, the drink that slakes thirst, the fire that warms cold, the cold that moderates heat, and, lastly, the common currency that buys all things, the balance and weight that equalizes the shepherd and the king, the simpleton and the sage.

Cervantes, Don Quixote, *1605*

The best things in life are nearest:
Breath in your nostrils, light in your
eyes, flowers at your feet, duties at your
hand, the path of right just before you.
Then do not grasp at the stars, but do
life's plain, common work as it comes,
certain that daily duties and daily
bread are the sweetest things in life.

Robert Louis Stevenson, 1850–1894

It was a gloriously beautiful
Scotch morning. The rain fell
softly and quietly.

Stephen Leacock, 1869–1944

Sunshine is delicious, rain is refreshing, wind braces us up, snow is exhilarating; there is really no such thing as bad weather, only different kinds of weather.

John Ruskin, 1819–1900

Man's life is but vain, for 'tis subject to pain
And sorrow and short as a bubble;
'Tis a hodge-podge of business
And money and care
And care and money and trouble.

But we'll take no care when the
Weather proves fair,
Nor will we now vex though it rain;
We'll banish all sorrow, and sing
Til tomorrow,
And angle and angle again.

Anon, c.1620

Our birth is but a sleep and a forgetting;
The soul that rises with us, our life's Star,
Hath had elsewhere its setting
And cometh from afar;
Not in entire forgetfulness,
And not in utter nakedness,
But trailing clouds of glory do we come
From God, who is our home:
Haven lies about us in our infancy!

William Wordsworth, 1770–1850
Ode on Intimations of Immortality

Love children especially, for like the angels they too are sinless, and they live to soften and purify our hearts, and, as it were, to guide us.

Fyodor Dostoyevsky, 1821–1881
The Brothers Karamazov

You were made for enjoyment, and the world was filled with things you will enjoy, unless you are too proud to be pleased by them, or too grasping to care for what you cannot turn to other account than mere delight.

John Ruskin, 1819–1900

And in the end,
it's not the years in your
life that count.
It's the life in your years.

Abraham Lincoln, 1784–1888

I find penguins at present the only comfort in life. One feels everything in the world so sympathetically ridiculous, one can't be angry when one looks at a penguin.

John Ruskin, 1819–1900

The great pleasure of a dog is that you may make a fool of yourself with him and not only will he not scold you, but he will make a fool of himself too.

Samuel Butler, 1835–1902

There are two
means of refuge
from the miseries of life:
music and cats.

Albert Schweitzer, 1875–1965

I gave my cat a bath the other day . . . He sat there, he enjoyed it, it was fun for me. The fur would stick to my tongue, but other than that . . ."

Steve Martin, 1945–

A bank is a place where they lend you an umbrella in fair weather and ask for it back when it begins to rain.

Robert Frost, 1874–1963

The chief value of money lies in the fact that one lives in a world in which it is overestimated.

H. L. Mencken, 1880–1956

Money can't buy you happiness but it does bring you a more pleasant form of misery.

Spike Milligan, 1918–2002

The man is richest
whose pleasures
are cheapest.

Henry David Thoreau, 1817–1862

Annual income twenty pounds,
annual income nineteen nineteen six,
result happiness.

Charles Dickens, 1812–1870

We act as though comfort and luxury were the chief requirements of life, when all that we need to make us really happy is something to be enthusiastic about.

Charles Kingsley, 1819–1875

Enthusiasm
is the greatest
asset in the world.
It beats money and power
and influence.

Henry Chester, 1850–1902

Money may be the husk of many things but not the kernel. It brings you food, but not appetite; medicine, but not health; acquaintance, but not friends; servants, but not loyalty; days of joy, but not peace or happiness.

Henrik Ibsen, 1828–1906

Ah, nowadays we are all of us so hard up, that the only pleasant things to pay are compliments. They're the only things we can pay.

Oscar Wilde, Lady Windemere's Fan

Excess on occasion is exhilarating.
It prevents moderation
from acquiring the deadening
effect of a habit.

Somerset Maugham, 1874–1965

You were made for enjoyment, and the world was filled with things you will enjoy, unless you are too proud to be pleased by them, or too grasping to care for what you cannot turn to other account than mere delight.

John Ruskin, 1819–1900

If you obey all the rules,
you miss all the fun.

Katherine Hepburn, 1907–2003

Never give in, never give in, never, never, never, never — in nothing, great or small, large or petty — never give in except to convictions of honour and good sense.

Winston Churchill, in a speech at Harrow School, 29th October 1941

Ever tried.
Ever failed.
No matter.
Try again.
Fail again.
Fail better.

Samuel Beckett, 1906–89, Westward Ho

Be joyful in hope,
patient in affliction,
patient in prayer.

The Bible, Romans *12.12*

What are days for?
Days are where we live.
They come, they wake us
Time and time over.
They are to be happy in:
Where can we live but days?

Philip Larkin, 1922–1985

It's never too late to become
what you might have been.

George Clooney, 1961–

Lead me not into temptation;
I can find the way myself

Rite Mae Brown, 1944–

Imperfection is beauty, madness is genius, and it is better to absolutely ridiculous than absolutely boring.

Marilyn Monroe, 1926–1962

May the road rise to meet you.
May the wind be always at your back.
May the sun shine warm upon your face,
And rains fall soft upon your fields.
And until we meet again
May God hold you in the hollow of
His hand.

Irish saying

Life is a matter of passing the time enjoyably. There may be other things in life, but I've been too busy passing my time enjoyably to think very deeply about them.

Peter Cook, 1937–1995

Don't underestimate the value of
Doing Nothing, of just going along,
listening to all the things you can't
hear, and not bothering.

Pooh's Little Instruction Book

I'm living so far beyond my income
that we may almost be said to be
living apart.

E. E. Cummings, 1894-1962

If they can make penicillin out of mouldy bread, they can sure make something out of you.

Muhammad Ali, 1942-

How do you define bliss?
You can't because it dwells in the mind's eye and is therefore individual. For me it's dogs, being by the sea, the laughter of children, coming home and love. Especially love. You need to define your own bliss and then seek it out, using every sense, every faculty at your disposal. If you don't then, by its very nature, it will pass you by.

Denise Robertson